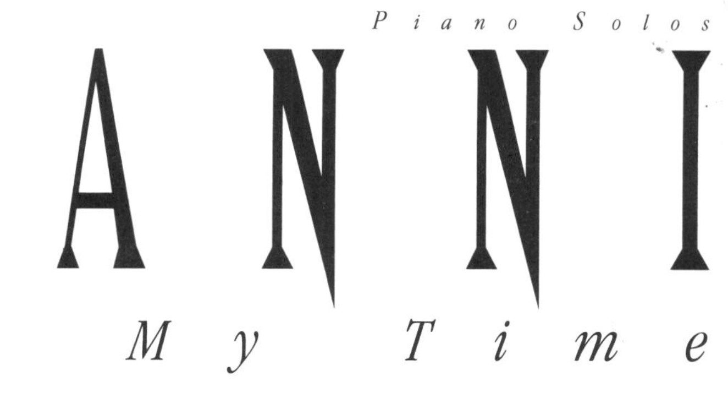

7777 West Bluemound Road P.O. Box 13819 Milwaukee, WI 53213

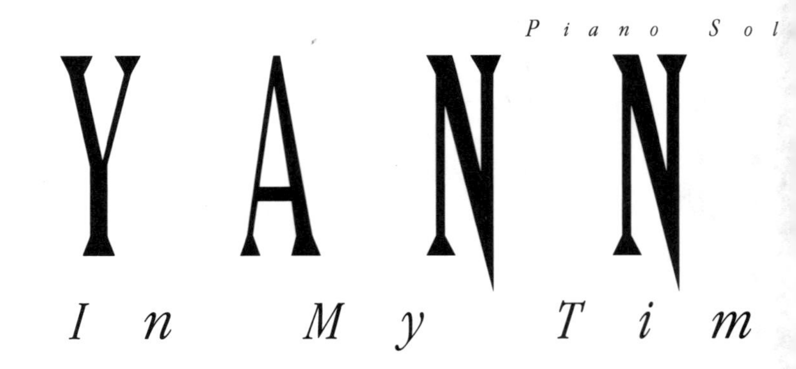

Transcriptions and Arrangements by Richard Boukas

Richard Boukas is a recognized New York recording artist, compos
author and educator. He currently tours with his Brazilian Jazz ense
ble, AMAZONA, whose CD for Jazz Essence is his third relea
Richard's other projects for Yanni include orchestral transcriptions
the Dallas Symphony Orchestra and piano arrangements for the pre
ous Hal Leonard book, "The Best Of Yanni."

B I O G R A P H Y

"Creativity is an inherent human quality of the highest order. When we create, we become more than the sum of our parts."

-Yanni-

"This internationally acclaimed composer, performer and recording artist has succeeded in presenting something new to contemporary audiences - music that celebrates the potential of the individual.

"I'm an optimist and a survivor," Yanni says, "and I put this in my music. It is my intention to share my emotions with the listener, but I also want to allow the listener to take this music and make it their own. The only way people can fully relate to it and enjoy it is when it means something in their life."

In the past five years, Yanni's music has been heard by more people in the U.S. than that of any other composer. The diversity of his work is apparent in his concert tours; his television themes and soundtracks, (including programming on all of the major networks); his movie scores; and, of course, his recordings.

His latest album, IN MY TIME, Yanni's ninth on Private Music, is his most open and intimate work to date. Using piano as the dominant instrument, the album is a departure from his previous works, but the Yanni "signature" is unmistakably present throughout. Here, he has created a timeless work presenting some of his most moving and eloquent themes.

"This was the kind of album I've been wanting to make for years," Yanni says, "a clear and honest album that would be consistent in its mood. I wanted the audience to feel the human being behind the music. One human being to another. For that reason, I intentionally kept the background instrumentation and production at a minimum."

Experiencing Yanni's music live is like experiencing it for the first time. Concert promoters credit Yanni's electrifying performances and innovative productions with bringing together audiences of traditional classics with the contemporar audience. About performing with symphony orchestras, he sa

"Symphonies can generate a tremendous amount of sound, beauty and emotion. That is part of their human feel and sweetness. Keyboards, on the other hand, give us access to millions of sounds. When I put the two together, the result is unique, and it's not only pleasing to the ear, but produces emotional responses that neither of the two can achieve on their own."

In concert, as in album sales, his music attracts a diverse following. It has become a common ground where generatio meet. From teens to the elderly, his fans represent a virtual melting pot of age groups and walks of life.

Yanni receives volumes of fan mail which thank him for the positive effect the music has had on their lives.

"My music heals me. It is the most valuable and unexpected g that I get in return for the effort of creating it. That it has a similar impact on the listener is very rewarding."

Yanni has secured a niche in television, particularly in the are of sports where his compositions have enhanced all of the majo events: Wide World of Sports, the Tour de France, World Figure Skating Championships, U.S. Open Tennis Championships, the World Series, and the Olympic Games. And, last year, he composed the theme for the ABC-TV nightly news program, "World News Now."

"The television programming happened on its own," he says. "Spontaneous combustion!"

Yanni has also achieved a successful film scoring career, creating the music for television movies such as ABC-TV's "I'll Take Romance" and "Nitti," CBS-TV's "I Love You Perfect" and "Children of the Bride," HBO's "Steal The Sky," Turner Broadcasting's "A Taste of Freedom," and the feature film "Heart of Midnight." He also collaborated with ex-Sex Pistols' manager, Malcolm McLaren, on a multiple-award winning British Airways commercial, and scored the music for a U.S. Government film biography of Pope John Paul II.

"The films are interesting to me. It's something I'll do for the rest of my life...a good exercise for me. It's like going to college."

Yanni actually did go to college. He has a Bachelor's Degree in Psychology from the University of Minnesota. Born in Kalamata, Greece, Yanni's musical talent - including "perfect pitch" and mastering the piano without lessons - became apparent early, though sport was also a prominent part of his life. (He is a former member of the Greek National Swimming Team and broke the national freestyle record at age 14.)

He explains his tendency to explore positive personal emotions: "There is so much music created today that expresses anger, and to some degree it's necessary. I choose not to do that. Rather, I try to inspire people and help them get in a frame of mind where they appreciate, and even enjoy, the world they live in...with all its problems!"

His DARE TO DREAM album (1992) went gold within two months of its release and has been nominated for a Grammy. The album was followed by a sell-out, 65-city concert tour which challenged audiences "not to be afraid to dream." His 1991 tour, aptly called "A Revolution in Sound," exemplified the fa that what Yanni has created in today's music/recording scene indeed, revolutionary.

His music refuses to be categorized. It is not jazz, classical or rock, Asian, Middle Eastern or European. Yet, Yanni fuses elements of all these into his music, resulting in forceful and uplifting orchestrations that are at once contemporary and classical. This approach is unusual, singular and remarkab individual.

Because he does not read or write the traditional language of music, Yanni uses a unique form of musical shorthand whic he invented as a youngster and still uses today. This is when composing skills were honed since, with no tape recorder or turntable at his disposal, the only way to play the songs he would hear on the radio or in the movies was to write the mu down in a format that would allow him to play it again on t piano. The process of hearing the music first in his mind an then translating it for the ear is an integral part of his creati expression when composing and helps explain his rare ability clearly express even the most subtle human emotions.

Yanni's musical approach is grounded in a philosophy where instrumental music conveys emotional messages unlimited lyrics or language.

"A simple word like 'happiness' can represent a range of emotions from taking a walk on a pleasant day to winning Super Bowl. Instrumental music, used correctly, is very dire and extremely accurate in describing even the most subtle human emotions. My music does not describe the circumstances, but how the circumstances make you feel. Since the music projects no gender, and there are no lyrics to interpreted, the listener can personalize it, and in a far mo precise way."

Yanni is currently riding a wave of achievement that erupted when REFLECTIONS OF PASSION, a collection of the most romantic themes from his previous five works, was released. The album (which continues to sell well) went platinum and stayed at the top of BILLBOARD's Adult Alternative Chart for a record-breaking 47 consecutive weeks. Its breakthrough sales success signaled that Yanni had arrived as a major creative force in the recording world.

"Creativity is no mystery. It's a matter of isolation and intense focus. You can't observe yourself creating...You have to become the music."

-Yanni-

BEFORE I GO

Composed by
YANNI

(poco rit. on repeat)
(arp. on repeat only)
(repeat only)
poco cresc.
accel. on repeat
(mf)
a tempo
1.
poco rit.
mp
mf

To Coda
rit.
2.
poco rit.
3
poco rit.

8va R.H.
p
loco
3
D.S. al Coda
CODA
decresc.
molto rit.
8va
Ethereally (♩ = 76)
sustained, cello-like
(keep pedal down)

(8va)
L.H.
R.H.
p
Ped.
Ped.
8va
(loco)
pp
Pedal al fine

ENCHANTMENT

Composed by
YANNI

(answer p)
mf
Concerto-like

With a sense of inevitability and forward motion
cresc. poco a poco
f
decresc.
2
2
mp

Gradual easing of tension
To Coda
1.
decresc. poco a poco
2
2
p
mp
2.
Hypnotically
p
mp/mf

cresc.
sub. mp
D.S. al Coda
CODA
2
2
Slower (♩ = 96)
p
pp

THE END OF AUGUST

Composed by
YANNI

mp
cresc.
More expressive
mf

More relaxed
(Take repeat on D.S.S. only)
mp
(Omit on D.S.)
1. Skip first 2 times and go directly to 2nd ending.
2.
cresc. poco a poco

mf
To Coda ⊕⊕
To Coda ⊕
D.S. al Coda
CODA
mp

D.S.S. al Coda
(take repeat)
CODA
rit.
2
3
p

FELITSA

Composed by
YANNI

Use pedal (with each change of harmony)

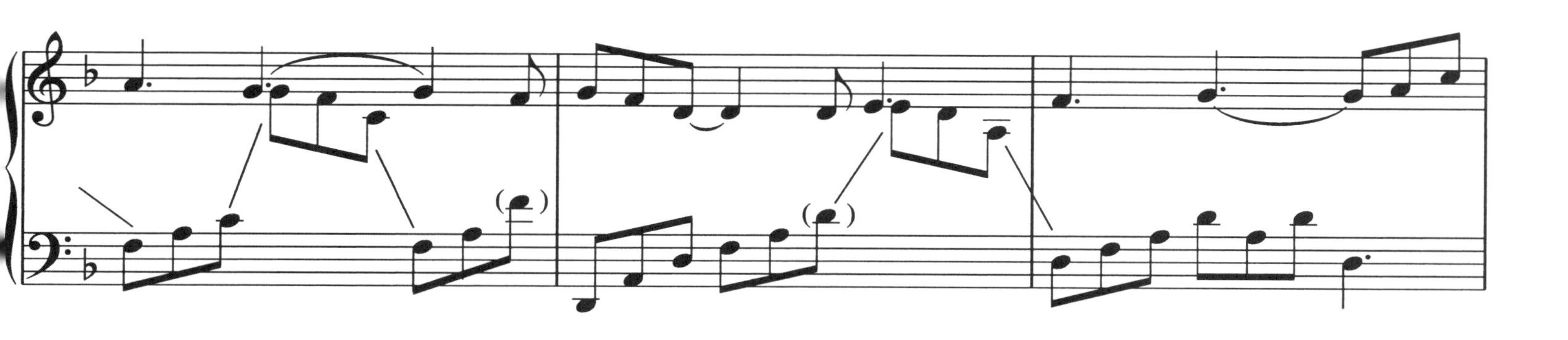

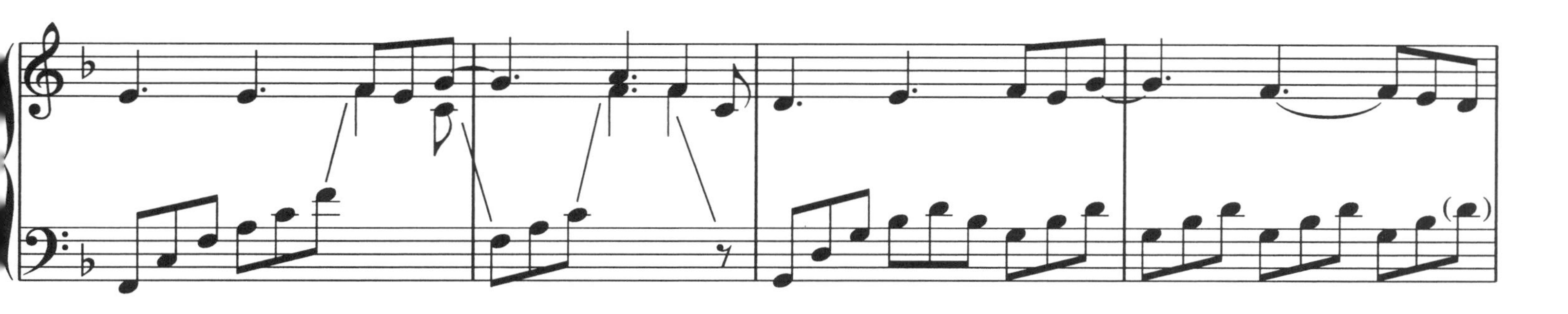

Jubilant, dancelike
mf
Lamenting, slightly distant
mp

cresc.
1.
D.S.
2.
To Coda
To Coda
decresc. poco a poco
D.S. al Coda
8va
mp
CODA
mp
mf

Singing, bright tone
D.S.S. al Coda
(R.H. loco)
decresc. poco a poco
CODA
mp
Somewhat resigned
mf

p
(answer)
Slower (𝅗𝅥 = 92)
3
3
8va
molto rit.
p

IN THE MORNING LIGHT

Composed by
YANNI

on D.C.
5
mf espressivo

With animation
mp
cresc. poco a poco
(al mf)
1.
poco rit.
D.C. al 2nd ending
2.
decresc.
8va
loco
Ped.

Delicately, with resolution
8va
p
mp
loco
decresc. molto rit.
pp

ONE MAN'S DREAM

Composed by
YANNI

R.H. 8va bassa on D.S.
D.S. loco
(answer mp)
mf

To Coda
(brief)
decresc.
p
From a distance
mp

8va
loco
cresc.
5
D.S. al Coda
mf
CODA
molto rit.
6
4
pp
4
4
Ped.
Slowly, fading
8va
loco
4
4
*

IN THE MIRROR

Composed by
YANNI

𝄋𝄋
poco rall.
cresc.
Play 3 times, 3rd time R.H. 8va
(D.S. take 2nd & 3rd endings)
(D.S.S. take 2nd ending)
(8va on D.S. and D.S.S. 2nd time)
𝄋
To Coda ⊕ ⊕
3
1,2
3
1,2

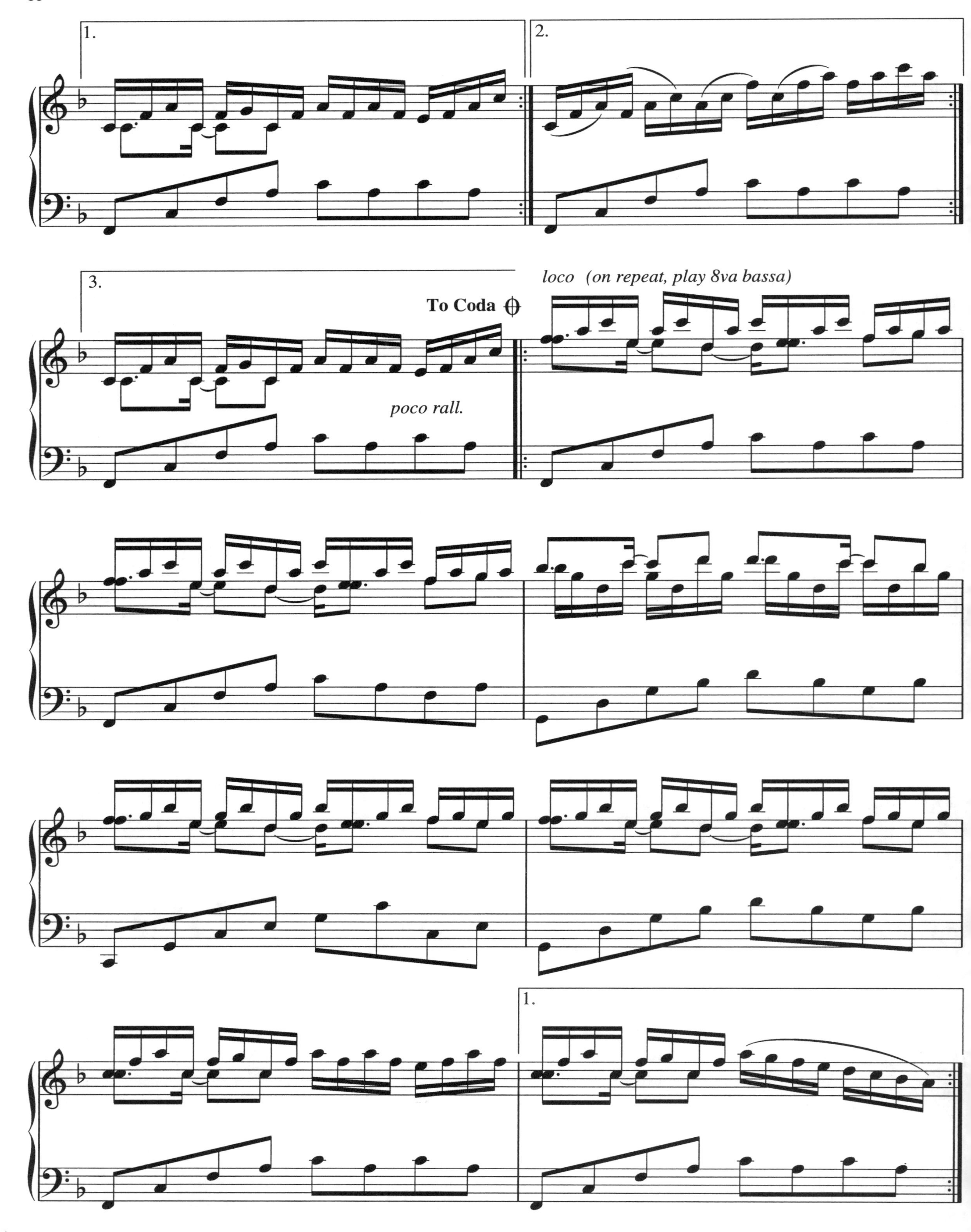
1.
2.
3.
To Coda
poco rall.
loco (on repeat, play 8va bassa)
1.

2.
D.S. al Coda
CODA
molto rit.
3
3
Start slowly, gradual accel. a tempo
p
cresc. poco a poco

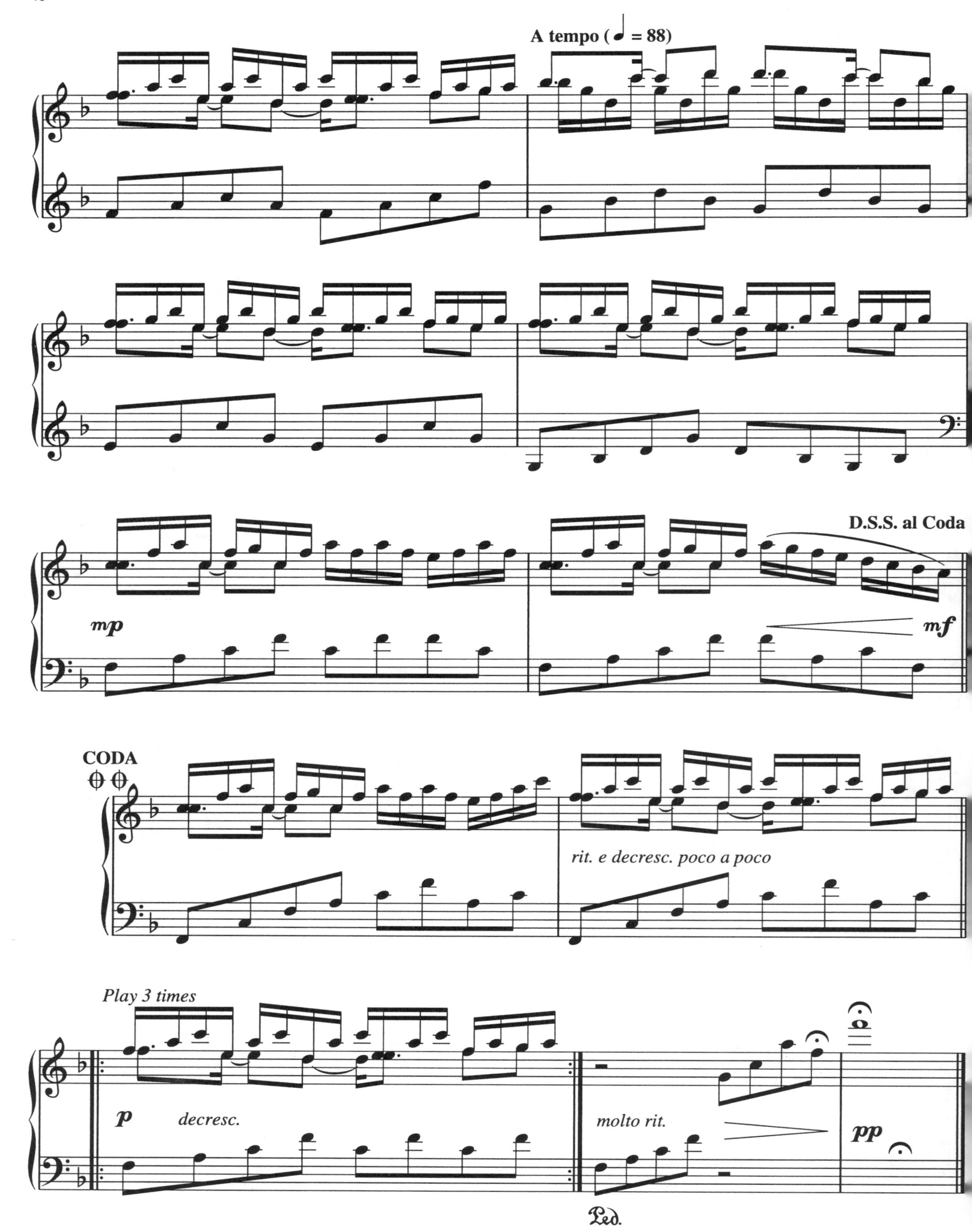

A tempo (♩ = 88)
mp
D.S.S. al Coda
mf
CODA
rit. e decresc. poco a poco
Play 3 times
p
decresc.
molto rit.
pp
Ped.

ONLY A MEMORY

Composed by
YANNI

With a flowing, relaxed spirit (♩ = 104)

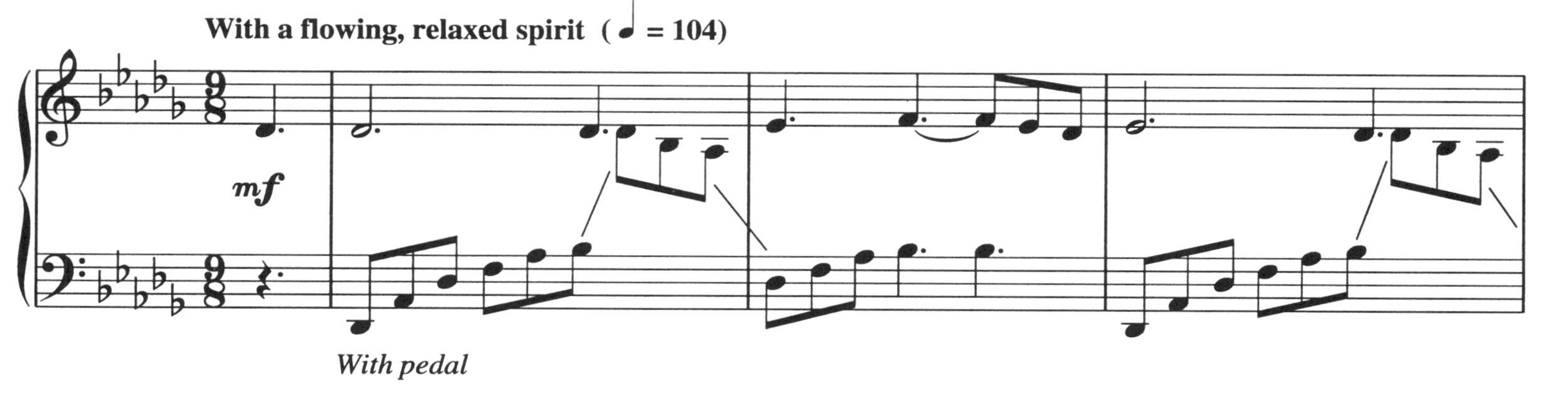

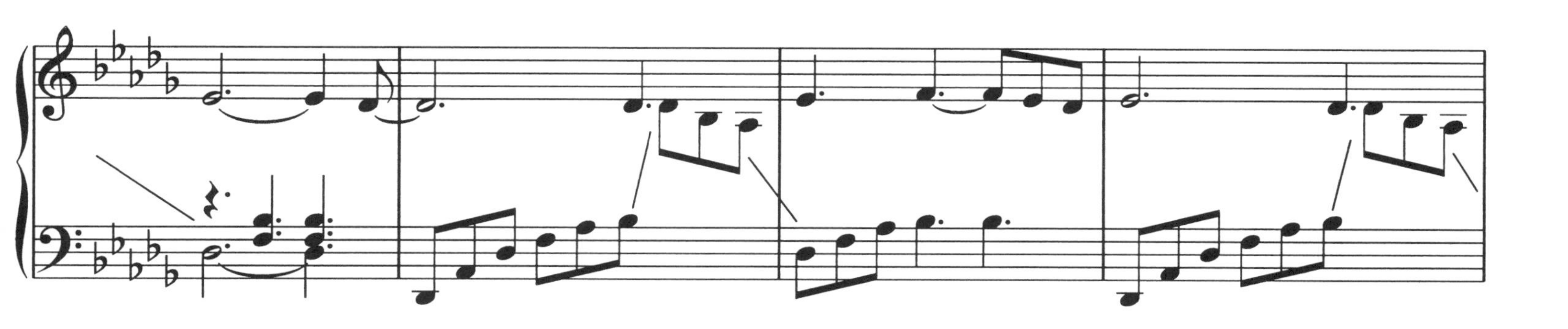

Folk-like, warm tone

3
mp
1.
mf

3
2.
decresc.
Ped.
Ped.
mp
mf
Less intense, innocently

cresc.
mf
decresc.
To Coda

mp
mf
R.H. 8va on repeat
legato
3
1.

2.
(8va)
loco

D.S. al Coda
CODA
mp fade slowly
decresc. poco a poco
Ped.
rit.
p
8va
molto rit.
pp
Ped. al fine

TO TAKE . . . TO HOLD

Composed by
YANNI

Evenly, peaceful (♩ = 116)

Stately, somewhat reserved

D.S. 2nd ending only
(tie on repeat only)
(tie on repeat only)
1.
2.
3
Expressively
mf
3
poco rall.
3
3

To Coda
3
Like intro
mp
3
(answer) p
mf
3
3
D.S. al Coda
CODA
3
mp
With a sense of
rising anticipation

mp - mf
1.
2.
cresc.
rit. poco a poco al fine
decresc.
p

WHISPERS IN THE DARK

Composed by
YANNI

3
Sweetly (♩ = 84)
loco
mf
a tempo
To Coda
3
With movement

(answer from afar)
pp
mp
(answer)
pp
Skip these two bars on D.S.S.

Skip these 2 bars 1st time, play on D.S.S.
(answer)
pp
To Coda
(answer)
pp
D.S. al Coda
CODA
3
3

cresc.
D.S.S. al Coda
3

CODA
pp (answer)
p
rit.
R.H.
pp
As intro (♩ = 72)
8va
3
Ped.
loco
ppp

UNTIL THE LAST MOMENT

Composed by
YANNI

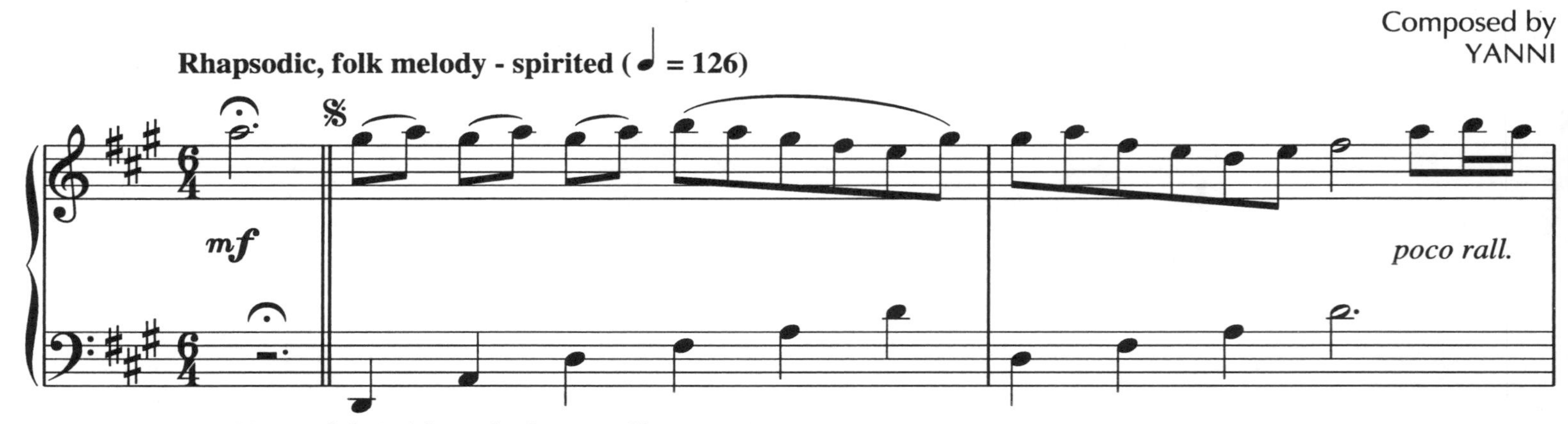

poco rall.
a tempo
cresc.
poco rall.

accel. poco a poco (to slightly faster than original tempo)
(On D.S., skip this measure)
poco rit.
Delicately (♩. = 66)
mp

With a Classical, Mozartean flair
cresc. poco a poco
With determination, stately
mf
D.S.
Sweeping, impassioned
3
D.S.

cresc.
Stately
Sweeping
3
To Coda

loco
ppp
mp
loco
D.S. al Coda
CODA
f
(♪. = ♪)
8va
loco
mf molto decresc.
mp
Ped. al Fine
Slowly
pp

8va
loco
decresc.
Ped.
Rubato (♩ = 58)
p
1.
(♩ = 104)
pp
2.
(♩ = 104)
8va
8va
pp
mp
(more present)
Mysteriously, from a distance
Middle Eastern spirit
With pedal
col 8va bassa